Francis Frith's
AROUND TRURO

◆

PHOTOGRAPHIC MEMORIES

Francis Frith's
AROUND TRURO

◆

Martin Dunning

FRITH
BOOK Co

First published in the United Kingdom in 2000 by
Frith Book Company Ltd

Hardback Edition 2000
ISBN 1-85937-147-7

Paperback Edition 2002
ISBN 1-85937-598-7

Reprinted in hardback 2002

British Library Cataloguing in Publication Data

Francis Frith's Around Truro
Martin Dunning

Frith Book Company Ltd
Frith's Barn, Teffont,
Salisbury, Wiltshire SP3 5QP
Tel: +44 (0) 1722 716 376
Email: info@francisfrith.co.uk
www.francisfrith.co.uk

Printed and bound in Great Britain

AS WITH ANY HISTORICAL DATABASE THE FRITH ARCHIVE IS CONSTANTLY BEING CORRECTED AND IMPROVED
AND THE PUBLISHERS WOULD WELCOME INFORMATION ON OMISSIONS OR INACCURACIES

Contents

FRANCIS FRITH: *Victorian Pioneer*

FRANCIS FRITH, Victorian founder of the world-famous photographic archive, was a complex and fascinating man. A devout Quaker and a highly successful Victorian businessman, he was both philosophic by nature and pioneering in outlook.

By 1855 Francis Frith had already established a wholesale grocery business in Liverpool, and sold it for the astonishing sum of £200,000, which is the equivalent today of over £15,000,000. Now a multi-millionaire, he was able to indulge his passion for travel. As a child he had pored over travel books written by early explorers, and his fancy and imagination had been stirred by family holidays to the sublime mountain regions of Wales and Scotland. 'What a land of spirit-stirring and enriching scenes and places!' he had written. He was to return to these scenes of grandeur in later years to 'recapture the thousands of vivid and tender memories', but with a different purpose. Now in his thirties, and captivated by the new science of photography, Frith set out on a series of pioneering journeys to the Nile regions that occupied him from 1856 until 1860.

INTRIGUE AND ADVENTURE

He took with him on his travels a specially-designed wicker carriage that acted as both dark-room and sleeping chamber. These far-flung journeys were packed with intrigue and adventure. In his life story, written when he was sixty-three, Frith tells of being held captive by bandits, and of fighting 'an awful midnight battle to the very point of surrender with a deadly pack of hungry, wild dogs'. Sporting flowing Arab costume, Frith arrived at Akaba by camel seventy years before Lawrence, where he encountered 'desert princes and rival sheikhs, blazing with jewel-hilted swords'.

During these extraordinary adventures he was assiduously exploring the desert regions bordering the Nile and patiently recording the antiquities and peoples with his camera. He was the first photographer to venture beyond the sixth cataract. Africa was still the mysterious 'Dark Continent', and Stanley and Livingstone's historic meeting was a decade into the future. The conditions for picture taking confound belief. He laboured for hours in his wicker dark-room in the sweltering heat of the desert, while the volatile chemicals fizzed dangerously in their trays. Often he was forced to work in remote tombs and caves where conditions were cooler. Back in London he exhibited his photographs and was 'rapturously cheered' by members of the Royal Society. His reputation as a photographer was made overnight. An eminent modern historian has likened their impact on the population of the time to that on our own generation of the first photographs taken on the surface of the moon.

VENTURE OF A LIFE-TIME

Characteristically, Frith quickly spotted the opportunity to create a new business as a specialist publisher of photographs. He lived in an era of immense and sometimes violent change. For the poor in the early part of Victoria's reign work was a drudge and the hours long, and people had precious little free time to enjoy themselves.

Most had no transport other than a cart or gig at their disposal, and had not travelled far beyond the boundaries of their own town or village. However, by the 1870s, the railways had threaded their way across the country, and Bank Holidays and half-day Saturdays had been made obligatory by Act of Parliament. All of a sudden the ordinary working man and his family were able to enjoy days out and see a little more of the world.

With characteristic business acumen, Francis Frith foresaw that these new tourists would enjoy having souvenirs to commemorate their days out. In 1860 he married Mary Ann Rosling and set out with the intention of photographing every city, town and village in Britain. For the next thirty years he travelled the country by train and by pony and trap, producing fine photographs of seaside resorts and beauty spots that were keenly bought by millions of Victorians. These prints were painstakingly pasted into family albums and pored over during the dark nights of winter, rekindling precious memories of summer excursions.

THE RISE OF FRITH & CO

Frith's studio was soon supplying retail shops all over the country. To meet the demand he gathered about him a small team of photographers, and published the work of independent artist-photographers of the calibre of Roger Fenton and Francis Bedford. In order to gain some understanding of the scale of Frith's business one only has to look at the catalogue issued by Frith & Co in 1886: it runs to some 670

pages, listing not only many thousands of views of the British Isles but also many photographs of most European countries, and China, Japan, the USA and Canada – note the sample page shown above from the hand-written *Frith & Co* ledgers detailing pictures taken. By 1890 Frith had created the greatest specialist photographic publishing company in the world, with over 2,000 outlets – more than the combined number that Boots and WH Smith have today! The picture on the right shows the *Frith & Co* display board at Ingleton in the Yorkshire Dales. Beautifully constructed with mahogany frame and gilt inserts, it could display up to a dozen local scenes.

POSTCARD BONANZA

The ever-popular holiday postcard we know today took many years to develop. In 1870 the Post Office issued the first plain cards, with a pre-printed stamp on one face. In 1894 they allowed other publishers' cards to be sent through the mail with an attached adhesive halfpenny stamp. Demand grew rapidly, and in 1895 a new size of postcard was permitted called the court card, but there was little room for illustration. In 1899, a year after Frith's death, a new card measuring 5.5 x 3.5 inches became the standard format, but it was not until 1902 that the divided back came into being, with address and message on one face and a full-size illustration on the other. *Frith & Co* were in the vanguard of postcard development, and Frith's sons Eustace and Cyril continued their father's monumental task, expanding the number of views offered to the public and recording more and more places in Britain, as the coasts and countryside were opened up to mass travel.

Francis Frith died in 1898 at his villa in Cannes, his great project still growing. The archive he created continued in business for another seventy years. By 1970 it contained over a third of a million pictures of 7,000 cities, towns and villages. The massive photographic record Frith has left to us stands as a living monument to a special and very remarkable man.

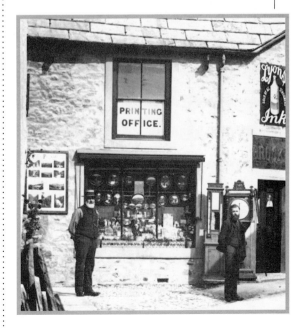

Frith's Archive: *A Unique Legacy*

FRANCIS FRITH'S legacy to us today is of immense significance and value, for the magnificent archive of evocative photographs he created provides a unique record of change in 7,000 cities, towns and villages throughout Britain over a century and more. Frith and his fellow studio photographers revisited locations many times down the years to update their views, compiling for us an enthralling and colourful pageant of British life and character.

We tend to think of Frith's sepia views of Britain as nostalgic, for most of us use them to conjure up memories of places in our own lives with which we have family associations. It often makes us forget that to Francis Frith they were records of daily life as it was actually being lived in the cities, towns and villages of his day. The Victorian age was one of great and often bewildering change for ordinary people, and though the pictures evoke an impression of slower times, life was as busy and hectic as it is today.

We are fortunate that Frith was a photographer of the people, dedicated to recording the minutiae of everyday life. For it is this sheer wealth of visual data, the painstaking chronicle of changes in dress, transport, street layouts, buildings, housing, engineering and landscape that captivates us so much today. His remarkable images offer us a powerful link with the past and with the lives of our ancestors.

TODAY'S TECHNOLOGY

Computers have now made it possible for Frith's many thousands of images to be accessed almost instantly. In the Frith archive today, each photograph is carefully 'digitised' then stored on a CD Rom. Frith archivists can locate a single photograph amongst thousands within seconds. Views can be catalogued and sorted under a variety of categories of place and content to the immediate benefit of researchers. Inexpensive reference prints can be created for them at the touch of a mouse button, and a wide range of books and other printed materials assembled and published for a wider, more general readership - in the next twelve months over a hundred Frith local history titles will be published! The

See Frith at www. frithbook.co.uk

day-to-day workings of the archive are very different from how they were in Francis Frith's time: imagine the herculean task of sorting through eleven tons of glass negatives as Frith had to do to locate a particular sequence of pictures! Yet the archive still prides itself on maintaining the same high standards of excellence laid down by Francis Frith, including the painstaking cataloguing and indexing of every view.

It is curious to reflect on how the internet now allows researchers in America and elsewhere greater instant access to the archive than Frith himself ever enjoyed. Many thousands of individual views can be called up on screen within seconds on one of the Frith internet sites, enabling people living continents away to revisit the streets of their ancestral home town, or view places in Britain where they have enjoyed holidays. Many overseas researchers welcome the chance to view special theme selections, such as transport, sports, costume and ancient monuments.

We are certain that Francis Frith would have heartily approved of these modern developments, for he himself was always working at the very limits of Victorian photographic technology.

THE VALUE OF THE ARCHIVE TODAY

Because of the benefits brought by the computer, Frith's images are increasingly studied by social historians, by researchers into genealogy and ancestory, by architects, town planners, and by teachers and schoolchildren involved in local history projects. In addition, the archive offers every one of

us a unique opportunity to examine the places where we and our families have lived and worked down the years. Immensely successful in Frith's own era, the archive is now, a century and more on, entering a new phase of popularity.

THE PAST IN TUNE WITH THE FUTURE

Historians consider the Francis Frith Collection to be of prime national importance. It is the only archive of its kind remaining in private ownership and has been valued at a million pounds. However, this figure is now rapidly increasing as digital technology enables more and more people around the world to enjoy its benefits.

Francis Frith's archive is now housed in an historic timber barn in the beautiful village of Teffont in Wiltshire. Its founder would not recognize the archive office as it is today. In place of the many thousands of dusty boxes containing glass plate negatives and an all-pervading odour of photographic chemicals, there are now ranks of computer screens. He would be amazed to watch his images travelling round the world at unimaginable speeds through network and internet lines.

The archive's future is both bright and exciting. Francis Frith, with his unshakeable belief in making photographs available to the greatest number of people, would undoubtedly approve of what is being done today with his lifetime's work. His photographs, depicting our shared past, are now bringing pleasure and enlightenment to millions around the world a century and more after his death.

AROUND TRURO – *An Introduction*

THE ANCIENT CORNISH city of Truro nestles in a deep valley at the head of one of the many branches of Cornwall's most important waterway, the Fal estuary. The history of the city and, indeed, its very existence, are inextricably linked with life on the river. In the old Cornish tongue - last spoken as a first language in the 19th century but still very much alive in the place names of the county - the name of Truro was 'Tri-veru', which translates as three rivers. Today, only two of the rivers - the Allen and the Kenwyn - are visible. The mysterious third river was more of a stream and has long since been forced underground, revealing itself today only where it comes out in a culvert just north-east of Boscawen Bridge. The rivers are Truro's raison d'être. In the times of the earliest settlement - which may have been as far back as Roman times - the valley would have provided shelter, and the then unpolluted waters of the rivers were rich in fish, shellfish and wildfowl. The valleys provided natural lines of communication inland, and to the south the estuary was a natural highway for produce and goods, eventually leading to the sea at what is now Falmouth.

The site is not without its disadvantages, however; modern roads into Truro all pass through deep cuttings, suggesting that the old highways must have been steep and treacherous, and the deep valleys, combined with the tides of the estuary, meant that the area was particularly prone to flooding. Nevertheless, the settlement flourished through a combination of farming, trade, and that most Cornish of commodities, tin.

In the Domesday Book, Truro is mentioned as comprising Great Truro and Little Truro, both under a fortress between the Kenwyn and the Allen, which was the seat of the Earls of Cornwall. An early incumbent was Richard de Lucy, who in 1140 was given the manor of Kenwyn by the King in return for his efforts in subduing a troublesome Cornish population. He presided over a settlement that had in 1130 been recognised as a borough and already had a powerful merchants' guild. The power of the merchants and burgesses was a reflection of the growing importance of Truro. Although far from the seat of power and the machinations of the court, the borough was wealthy and held a trump card in tin. The town's status was recognised in 1295 when it was invited to send two Members of Parliament to the Model Parliament. The journey for these two stout souls must have been daunting; on today's roads the distance is 270 miles, but in 1295 the journey would have been far longer and probably took months.

The town continued to grow. Ships traded from the port out into the English Channel and beyond, and river barges attended to local trade around the estuary, navigating the Tresillian River, the Fal, Restronguet Creek and a host of other small creeks and inlets, carrying people, goods, timber and grain. Mills, powered by water drawn off the rivers in leats and used for grinding corn and fulling cloth, sprang up all round the town: Carvedras, Pool Mills, Moresk, Coosebean, Calenick and Trennick to name but a few.

In 1327 Edward II proclaimed Truro a Stannary town, giving it the official duty of testing and stamping tin. An important boost to the town's status and trade, this did have another side: stamping meant that for the first time a record of tin production was being kept, which therefore allowed the King to levy taxes and duties more effectively. As a result, some enterprising businessmen took to smuggling; by Elizabethan times it has been estimated that as much as 75% of tin production was being smuggled to avoid duties. The Coinage Hall was built in 1351 to provide a centre for the assaying and stamping of tin, but despite the strength of trade the town was in dire straits. The Black Death had swept through Cornwall and in 1349 had decimated Truro. The town went into a decline: a survey in 1413 showed that Truro was underpopulated, decaying, depressed and prone to flooding. The waterside was polluted and stinking, rats and wild dogs abounded, cholera and smallpox were rife, and the burgesses could

THE CATHEDRAL c1910 23921A

no longer meet the monarch's demands for taxes and tithes.

The inhabitants struggled on, for adversity was nothing new in Cornwall, and gradually Truro recovered. In 1589 Queen Elizabeth granted the town its charter with a mayor, four aldermen and 20 burgesses. Documents of the time reveal that there were concerns in 1620 Truro was granted a coat of arms with the motto Exaltatum Cornu In Deo ('Mine horn is exalted in the Lord'). Both the coat of arms and the town seals show ships and fish, another indication of the importance of the rivers. Other trades were developing. The estuary has long been known for its shellfish, and the inhabitants of St Clement were pick-

MALPAS, THE RIVER 1890 24145

about the future of the port; where, a hundred years before, vessels of 100 tons regularly came to the head of the estuary, silting of the river now limited navigation to vessels of thirty tons. The culprit was waste from the mines; Truro was being stifled by its own success, a fate that befell other south-west tin ports such as Plympton. Ships now often anchored at Malpas to load their cargoes into smaller barges for the last few miles to Truro.

Trade continued in spite of the silting, and ling oysters in quart barrels to send to the West Indies. Oysters seem to have been a major commodity: it was not unusual for rent for a property to include '200 of oysters per annum' as a term of the lease.

The Civil War brought about another change in fortunes for the town. Like the rest of Cornwall, Truro was staunchly Royalist, but while the garrison of Pendennis Castle at nearby Falmouth held out for months against Parliamentarian forces led by Fairfax, Truro was not so easy to defend, and the Royalist commander Sir Ralph Hopton surrendered to Fairfax at Tresillian Bridge in 1646. The bravery of Sir John Arundel's forces at Falmouth, set against Truro's apparent acquiescence, had grave repercussions upon the restoration of the monarchy. Charles II came to the throne in 1660; in 1661, remembering the town's loyalty to his father, he granted Falmouth its charter. Truro had held rights over the estuary as far south as Black Rock in Falmouth harbour, and had therefore been able to raise dues on shipping, but as part of Falmouth's charter it received many of Truro's river rights, which were never to be restored despite efforts in the courts by the burgesses of Truro.

In the early 18th century starving miners marched on Truro, and in 1752 the Stannary Parliament, which looked after the interests of miners, sat for the last time. Stagecoaches started running between Torpoint and Truro, giving the town a regular link at last with the rest of the country, and mine owners such as the Lemons, the Daniells and the Enys grew richer and more powerful and built smelting works, such as those at Calenick, and fine houses like the old Mansion House on Quay Street. Boscawen Street thrived and the magnificent Georgian terrace of Lemon Street was built, and in 1846 City Hall was constructed - a fine example of Victorian civic pride.

Recognised as the administrative centre of the county as well as a centre of trade and industry, and stimulated by the arrival of the railway in 1859, Truro now set about raising its status yet again. It had long irked Truronians that matters ecclesiastical were administered from far-distant Exeter, and a vigorous lobbying campaign began. This eventually bore fruit with an announcement in the London Gazette: 'The Queen has been pleased by Letters Patent under the Great Seal of the United Kingdom bearing the date 28th day of August 1877, to ordain and declare that the Borough of Truro, in the County of Cornwall shall be a city, and shall be called and styled 'the City of Truro in the County of Cornwall". Construction of the new cathedral, dedicated to the Blessed Virgin Mary and the first to be built in England for 800 years, began in 1880 and continued for thirty years. City status and the building of the cathedral gave a boost to Truro; another building boom ensued, driven by the architect Sylvanus Trevail, whose taste for the Baroque and red brick can be seen all round the city.

The mines were in decline, and the sight of schooners moored at the quayside was becoming less common. The last Truro-owned ship, the Mary Barrow, went down off the Isle of Man in 1936; while Falmouth, with its deepwater anchorage and extensive docks, flourished as a port, Truro, inland and slowly silting up, saw less and less trade on the river. Coasters called until the 1960s with timber and coal, but now the river traffic is limited to pleasure boats.

Truro has moved on from its dependence on the rivers and is now a thriving city, county town of Cornwall, with a bustling shopping centre and the new Crown Court, built in 1988 to much acclaim in a modernist style but with classical elements which would no doubt have pleased Sylvanus Trevail. The three great spires of the Cathedral still dominate the little city in the valley, confirmation in granite of what Truronians have known for centuries - that their city is truly the capital of Cornwall.

DEVORAN, THE VILLAGE c1955 D120001
Devoran lies at the head of Restronguet Creek and about ten miles as the oarsman paddles downstream from Truro. The cars in this picture are local - 'CV' is a Cornish registration and 'JY' a Plymouth one.

DEVORAN, THE VILLAGE c1955 D120002
Although quiet today, the streets of Devoran were bustling in the 19th century when the mineral railway arrived, bringing copper and tin from the mines inland to load aboard the many schooners that moored in the creek.

DEVORAN, GENERAL VIEW C1955 D120005

Devoran's prosperity was short-lived. In 1850 there were five trains a day and as many as 30 ships in port, but by 1870 the mines were declining and soon the village reverted to being a backwater.

FEOCK, LOE BEACH 1936 87516

This view looks south-east to the mouth of the little creek that runs out to the main estuary from Feock. To the left the Fal runs up to Truro some seven miles upstream; downstream are the Carrick Roads and Falmouth.

FEOCK, LOE BEACH 1936 87519
This view looks back up the creek towards Feock. Anchored left is a wooden, gaff-rigged working boat of the type that was once so common in Cornish harbours and rivers. Sturdy and seaworthy, they were used for fishing and for transporting both people and cargo.

FEOCK
The Post Office 1936
The Western National bus timetables - in the company livery of green with gold lettering and with the poster in pale yellow - were once a common sight all over Devon and Cornwall, and buses for small villages such as Feock were more frequent in the thirties than they are today.

◆

FEOCK
Churchtown 1936
Feock has been predominantly a farming community, apart from a period in the 18th and 19th centuries when mining and the presence of a smelter at nearby Penpol brought miners and sailors - and, for a time, the Redruth and Chacewater Railway.

FEOCK, THE POST OFFICE 1936 87529

FEOCK, CHURCHTOWN 1936 87532

FEOCK, THE VILLAGE c1955 F17010

Life during Feock's brief period of prosperity seems to have been somewhat rumbustious - apparently, drinkers used to dip their mugs into a tin bath filled with liquor (probably smuggled 'Cousin Jackie' or brandy) and continued to do so until the bath was dry. Today, Feock is tranquil and does not even have a pub.

FEOCK, THE CHURCH TOWER 1936 87539

This 13th-century church tower stands some way from the 19th-century church of St Feoca, now the parish church. This was a fishermen's church, where they used to pray before putting out to sea. It was also the place where the last sermon in the Cornish tongue was preached.

KING HARRY PASSAGE 1890 23951
The King Harry Ferry takes its name from the chapel dedicated to Our Lady and King Henry that once stood on the Tolverne bank near where this picture was taken.

KING HARRY PASSAGE, THE PIER 1890 24147
Another story says that King Henry VI once swam across the river here, hence the name of King Harry Passage. History does not record whether he swam back again, but whatever the case he must have been a strong swimmer.

KING HARRY PASSAGE
The Ferry-Boats 1890 24148
This must have been one of the last of the old style
ferries, embarking horses, carriages, passengers and
luggage on a precarious platform atop a rowing boat.
Crossings had to take place at slack water to ensure
reaching the opposite bank safely.

TRELISSICK, KING HARRY FERRY c1955 T209001
Five miles inland from Falmouth, King Harry Passage is the lowest point on the estuary where vehicles can cross, shortening the road journey from Falmouth to St Mawes by nearly 20 miles.

TRELISSICK, KING HARRY FERRY c1955 T209004
A ferry is known to have existed here since 1649, but steam-driven chain ferries did not start running until 1899. Previous ferries were hampered by the strong tides that run in the estuary, but chain ferries can run at any state of the tide.

TRELISSICK, SHIPPING ON THE RIVER c1955 T209006
Ships mothballed in the sheltered part of the estuary above Turnaware Point are still a common sight. In the 1930s, ships were moored five abreast from Woodbury just downstream of Malpas to Turnaware Point.

OLD COTTAGES 1890 23961
These are typical Cornish cottages - walls of local stone (in this case probably slate), and thatched roofs. The brick chimneys probably indicate that these were occupied by somebody who had moved at least one rung up the ladder from the status of labourer or farmhand.

TREGOTHNAN, THE BOAT HOUSE 1890 23959
Dances were once held in the top floor of the boathouse for guests of Lord Falmouth, who were transported here by Jenny Mopus, who operated the Malpas Ferry at the end of the 18th century and the beginning of the 19th century.

TREGOTHNAN HOUSE 1890 23958
Tregothnan ('place of the twisting brook') is the family seat of the Boscawen family, who hold the title of Lord Falmouth. Despite its almost Elizabethan appearance (all those chimneys!) the house was in fact completed in 1822.

TREGOTHNAN HOUSE 1890 23957
Upon completion of Tregothnan, Lord Falmouth celebrated by presenting fatted oxen to the parishioners of Kenwyn, Kea and Truro.

TREGOTHNAN LODGE 1890 23956
This entrance to the Tregothnan estate lies just off the A39 at Tresillian, some four miles from the house itself. Tregothnan is in the parish of St Michael Penkevil, and the church is half a mile from the house.

THE TREGOTHNAN LANDING PLACE 1890 23954

In the distance, hidden behind the trees, the river splits: the right-hand branch goes down to Falmouth, and the left to Ruan Lanihorne. Tregothnan actually lies on the Truro River, which is a tributary of the Fal.

VIEW NEAR TREGOTHNAN 1890 23952

Anchored in the background (and beached in photograph No 23954) is one of the many barges that until the middle of the 20th century were the workhorses of the estuary, carrying anything from grain to timber.

THE RIVER FAL 1890
Taken from near Tolverne, this photograph shows the Tregothnan boathouse on the opposite bank and, on the skyline just to the left of the boathouse, Tregothnan House itself.

VIEW FROM MALPAS 1890
On the point opposite, the building to the left of the road is the old Ship Inn, which flourished from 1774-1852, and to its right, the ferryman's cottage. Malpas takes its name from the French 'Mal Pas' meaning bad road, as it can be a treacherous passage when windy.

THE RIVER FAL 1890 24149

VIEW FROM MALPAS 1890 24143

CALENICK, THE VILLAGE 1912 64745
Calenick was the site of a smelting works, founded by the Lemon and Daniel families, and operated from 1710-1891. This cottage, at the foot of School Hill, was demolished in 1925.

MALPAS, THE RIVER 1890 24145
Ships often anchored here to offload Truro-bound cargo into barges. Visible on the Malpas shore is the Scoble and Davies shipbuilding yard, where many local ships were built. The biggest was the 'Malpas Belle', the only Truro-built vessel to round Cape Horn.

ST CLEMENT'S, THE CHURCH 1890 23948
St Clement's lies a couple of miles south-east of Truro on the bank of the Tresillian River. The church was that of the Duchy Manor of Moresk, and the slate-hung building above the lych gate, just left of the magnolia tree, was the schoolroom.

ST CLEMENT'S, THE CHURCH AND COTTAGES 1890 23949
The Ship Inn, on the left, was in business from 1844 until 1908. Its last landlord was Thomas Andrew, and it is now a private house.

ST CLEMENT'S, THE VILLAGE 1912 64739
Unmade roads, no cars, no overhead power lines and no television aerials - but the streetlight (left) has made its entrance. The road on the right leads down to the river.

ST CLEMENT'S, THE VILLAGE 1912 64740

The left-hand house (behind the wooden shed) later became the Post Office. Until World War Two, a favourite form of fishing here was 'hacking', where nets were strung across the full width of the river from a boat, and at low tide the villagers would brave the mud to retrieve mullet, flounder, dab and bream.

ST CLEMENT'S, THE CHURCH 1890 23950

St Clement's church dates from the 14th century, although it has been much altered. Outside the south wall stands the ancient Ignioc Stone, thought to date from AD500, which until 1938 was in use as a gatepost at the vicarage.

TRESILLIAN, THE VILLAGE c1955 T210004
Tresillian was once an important port and a favoured haunt for smugglers. However, waste from mineworkings upstream led to the river silting up and becoming unnavigable, although barges did call here until 1900. In the background are the gates to the Tregothnan estate.

TRESILLIAN, THE BRIDGE c1955 T210001
There has been a bridge at Tresillian since 1309. Somewhere near here, on 10 March 1646, the Royalist leader Sir Ralph Hopton met with the Parliamentarian leader Fairfax. Two days later they signed a treaty at Truro which effectively ended the Civil War.

TRESILLIAN, THE VILLAGE C1955 T210006

TRESILLIAN
The Village c1955

In the background, indicated by the ships' wheels, is the Wheel Inn, whose landlords go back as far as 1770. The A39 bears right after the inn towards Tresillian Bridge.

PROBUS
The Church c1955

The 15th-century church of St Probus has the highest tower of any church in Cornwall save Truro Cathedral. Probus was once one of the richest parishes in the county, supporting a dean, five prebendaries, a vicar and two chaplains.

PROBUS, THE CHURCH C1955 P247001

FROM THE VIADUCT 1890 23919
Cornwall was once part of the Church of England Diocese of Exeter, but in the 19th century the growing prosperity of the county because of mining meant that it was granted its own diocese - that of Truro - which was established in 1876.

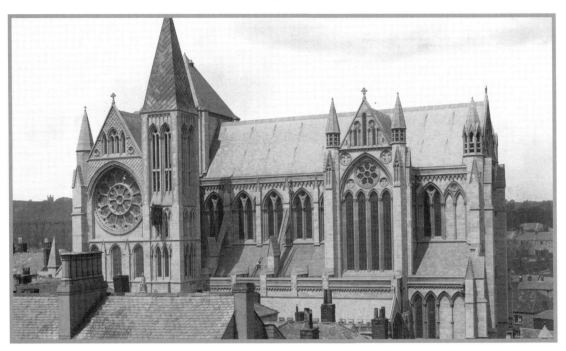

THE CATHEDRAL 1890 23921
The Cathedral was built on the site of the old parish church of Truro, St Mary's, which was in poor repair. St Mary's is still the parish church, within the cathedral, and distinguished by its copper-clad spire, visible at centre left.

THE CATHEDRAL FROM THE MILL POOL 1890 23923
Although built in the Early English Gothic style, construction of the cathedral did not start until 1880, when the foundation stone was laid by the Prince of Wales, later to become Edward VII. This view is from the north, and taken before the addition of the west front and the great central tower.

THE CATHEDRAL 1890 23924
Building stone for the Cathedral came from many sources, near and far. The main stonework of Cornish granite came from Mabe and St Stephen, and the mouldings, dressings and vaults are made from Corsham stone and Doulting stone from Somerset.

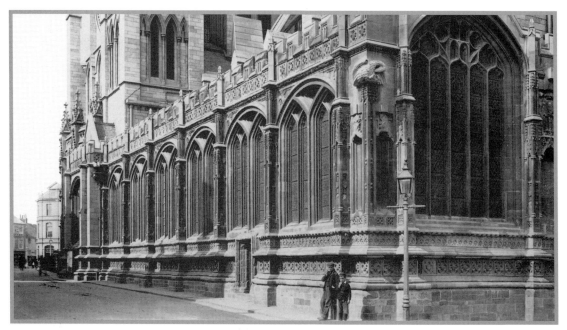

THE CATHEDRAL 1895 37059

This photograph shows the original carved stonework of St Mary's, preserved during the building of the cathedral and incorporated as St Mary's aisle. The crenellated parapet and carvings date from the 16th century, and its weathering contrasts with the smooth Victorian stonework of the rest of the cathedral.

THE CATHEDRAL, NAVE WEST 1903 49914

Above the doors at the west end of the nave are statues of those involved in the establishment of the Cathedral - Queen Victoria, Edward VII, Queen Alexandra, George V and several bishops. The architect John Pearson intended to design a Cathedral that would 'bring people to their knees soonest'.

THE CATHEDRAL, NAVE EAST 1903 50795
The Benediction of the nave took place on 15 July 1903 with the Prince and Princess of Wales, later King George V and Queen Mary, in attendance. After the ceremony they departed with Lord Falmouth for a short stay at Tregothnan.

THE CATHEDRAL, THE WAR MEMORIAL 1903 50795A
This memorial commemorates Cornishmen who died in the Boer war in South Africa in 1899-1902. The Duke of Cornwall's Light Infantry was the county regiment, and in the Charge of Paardeburg sustained 25% casualties, an act of bravery which was widely commended.

THE CATHEDRAL c1910 23921A
The central tower reaches a height of 250 feet and was
completed in 1903 as a memorial to Queen Victoria.
In the foreground are the masts of some of the many
schooners that used to visit Truro.

THE CATHEDRAL, WEST FRONT c1910 23930A
The twin towers of the west front were completed in 1910. They are 204 feet high and are somewhat unusual for Cornwall, in that they have spires. The north-west tower has a peal of ten bells.

THE BISHOP'S PALACE 1890 23944
The original Bishop's Palace was this fine Georgian mansion which had been the vicarage at Kenwyn. It is now a preparatory school.

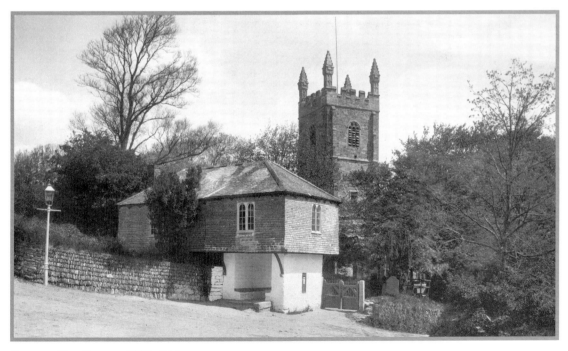

KENWYN, THE CHURCH 1890 23947
Kenwyn Church was originally consecrated in 1259; it was extended in the 15th century and restored in the 19th century. The slate-hung lych gate is typical of the area.

THE CHAIN WALK 1895 37060B
This was for many years a favourite walk for Truronians taking a stroll northwards out of town. The walk still exists, but the green fields on the right are now home to a housing estate.

THE CATHEDRAL FROM THE LEATS 1911 63706
This picture was taken shortly after the completion of the cathedral, the first new one to have been built in England for over 800 years. The first Bishop was Dr Edward White Benson.

FROM LEMON BRIDGE 1898 41637A

On the left is Back Quay, and on the right Lemon Quay, which was covered over in 1923 to form a car park. The site of N Gill and Son is now occupied by Woolworths.

TRURO COLLEGE FROM THE BRIDGE 1890 24133

Sailing barges such as those moored here were a common sight in Truro until World War Two. Up to 40 of them, each of 40-80 tons, worked the river, often carrying cargo from schooners that had unloaded at Malpas. On the horizon is Truro College, now Truro School.

THE CATHEDRAL FROM THE RIVER 1903 50854B

The building with the arched doorway, centre left, was once the Fighting Cocks Inn, birthplace of Richard Lander (whose father was the landlord) and now the site of a shopping arcade. The area in front of it was a bowling green, and behind the Inn can be seen the clock tower of the City Hall.

THE BRIDGE AND THE LOCK GATES c1955 T86041

Boscawen Bridge was opened in 1862; it was by-passed in the 1960s when Morlaix Avenue was built. W Penrose and Son were sailmakers who later made and hired tents, including what was at the time the biggest tent in the world.

THE HARBOUR c1955 T86027
Garras Wharf was often occupied by schooners such as the 'Lizzie', the 'Bessie' and the 'Mary Barrow'. The latter was the last Truro-owned ship, and went down off the Isle of Man in 1936.

THE QUAY SIDE c1955 T86023

Until the 1960s the Truro River was being regularly dredged, and coasters such as the 'Narwhal' were frequent visitors. They carried coal (a pile of which can be seen on the wharf at right), fruit, timber and all sorts of other cargoes.

QUAY STREET c1960 T86051

On the right is the Old Mansion House, built in 1709 by Samuel Enys, one of a long line of Enys who were prominent local land and mine owners. It is a good example of a Cornish town house of the period. On the left is the Palace Theatre and the Dolphin Buttery.

GENERAL VIEW 1890 24129

Truro nestles in the valleys of the River Kenwyn and the River Allen; they meet below the Cathedral to form the Truro River, which in turn joins the river Fal south of Tregothnan.

ST GEORGE'S ROAD AND THE CHURCH 1911 63707

The Anglican Church of St George on St George's Road was built in 1855, and has a very high roof with scissor-braces and wind-braces. In the background is the new viaduct, built in 1902 to replace Brunel's original, the piers of which still stand.

BOSCAWEN PARK 1912 64735

Boscawen Park was established by Truro City Council in 1900 around the pool that was once the mill pond of Trennick Mill. The tennis courts were opened by the Mayor, E J Lodge, in 1923.

WATERFALL GARDENS 1898 41636

Waterfall Gardens were donated in 1893 by Edward Goodridge Heard, who was Mayor from 1872-3. They are on the site of the old pigeon house of St Dominic's Friary. The wooded viaduct was built in 1859.

THE CATHEDRAL FROM THE SQUARE 1938 88956
Buses from Truro travelled to all parts of the county; the ones gathered here are going to Falmouth, Perranporth, and Newquay. The Western National enquiries office is on the right of the picture.

THE LANDER COLUMN 1890

The Lander monument in Upper Lemon Villas commemorates Truro-born explorers Richard and John Lander, who discovered the source of the Niger. The statue on top (added in 1852) is of Richard.

LEMON STREET c1955

Richard Lander had a short but action-packed life. Born in 1804, he had his first taste of travel at the age of 11 when he went to the West Indies. Later he joined his brother John to explore Africa, and named an island on the River Niger 'Truro'. He died after being wounded by natives in 1834.

THE LANDER COLUMN 1890 23946

LEMON STREET c1955 T86026

UPPER LEMON STREET 1890 24132
Lemon Street consists of 18th- and 19th-century
buildings, and is considered to be one of the finest
examples of a complete Georgian street in England.
Three years after this picture was taken, John Julian
and Company suffered a serious fire.

LEMON STREET c1955 T86022

At the top of the hill the cupola of the Anglican church of St John, built in 1828, is just visible. The slender Tuscan columns supporting the cupola are made of wood. The Plaza Cinema was built in 1935 and still stands.

LEMON STREET c1955 T86025

Lemon Street's fine Georgian terrace was built from Bath stone donated by Ralph Allen. Allen was a friend of the 18th-century writers Alexander Pope and Henry Fielding, who based his character Squire Allworthy on Allen.

THE RED LION HOTEL C 1955
One of Truro's best-loved buildings, the Red Lion was originally a private mansion, but became a hotel in 1671 when it rejoiced under the name of 'Mr Foote's Guest House'. The name changed to the Red Lion in 1769.

LEMON STREET C1955
14 July 1967 was a sad day for Truronians: a lorry coming down Lemon Street suffered brake failure and it careered out of control into the Red Lion, which was so badly damaged that it had to be demolished.

THE RED LION HOTEL C 1955 T86020

LEMON STREET C1955 T86028

KING STREET 1897 40594
The imposing, Baroque-influenced Barclays Bank
building (centre), with its columns, cornices and
finials, was built in the late 19th century.

BOSCAWEN STREET 1897 40591
Boscawen Street takes its name from that of the family of Lord Falmouth. In the background, decorators are working on some extremely long ladders which would probably give a modern Health and Safety inspector kittens!

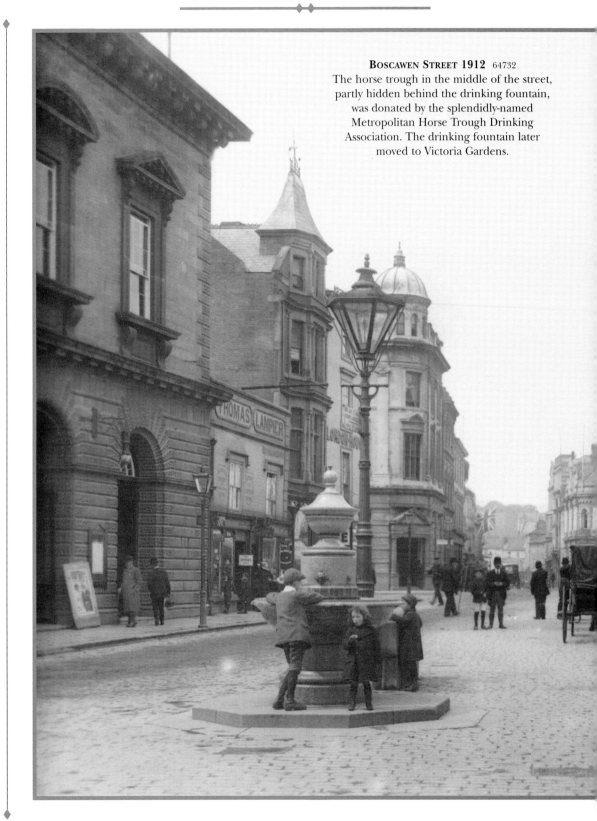

BOSCAWEN STREET 1912 64732
The horse trough in the middle of the street,
partly hidden behind the drinking fountain,
was donated by the splendidly-named
Metropolitan Horse Trough Drinking
Association. The drinking fountain later
moved to Victoria Gardens.

BOSCAWEN STREET 1923 73616
It is only eleven years on from photograph No 64732, and the motor car has almost completely replaced the horse. The curious little wheeled shed on the left of the picture is a cabman's shelter, built by the National Cabman's Shelter Association.

BOSCAWEN STREET 1923 73618
Webb and Co was founded by John Webb and stayed in the family until grandson John Webb died in the polio epidemic of 1949. Despite the ascendancy of the motor car, horses remained in use. Here, in the background, is a horse-drawn removals wagon owned by Pickfords.

BOSCAWEN STREET 1923 73617
The prominent gabled building in the centre was built
on the site of the old Coinage Hall, where tin was
tested and taxed. The hall was pulled down in 1844
and replaced by Tweedy's Bank.

BOSCAWEN STREET 1940 88960
Pearson's Jewellers and Opticians (left) moved to
Lemon Quay in about 1950 and closed in 1970.
J Roberts Women's Outfitters often sponsored
charity fashion shows in the City Hall; they remain
a family business, still on Boscawen Street.

BOSCAWEN STREET 1940 88959
The cupola (top left) belongs to the Lloyd's bank building, which stands at the junction of Boscawen Street and Lemon Street. It was designed by the ubiquitous Sylvanus Trevail, architect of many Cornish buildings including the famous Headland Hotel in Newquay.

BOSCAWEN STREET c1955 T86017
Spot the familiar high-street names: Burton's the Tailors, Oliver's shoes, Boots the Chemist and Lyons Swiss Rolls. Despite the preponderance of cars, there still appears to be a horse-drawn carriage outside Boots.

BOSCAWEN STREET c1955 T86018
The prominent clock-tower is that of the City Hall, built in 1846 in the Italian Renaissance style. In 1914 the Hall suffered a disastrous fire, but it was rebuilt, with a new clock given by an anonymous donor.

BOSCAWEN STREET c1955 T86009
To the left of the Red Lion is the National Provincial Bank. The premises were previously occupied by Farrow's Bank, which collapsed in 1920 and was taken over by the National Provincial.

BOSCAWEN STREET c1955 T86021
Many of the buildings on Boscawen Street date from the 18th and 19th centuries. Originally houses, they are now shops and business; although their frontages have changed in accordance with high street trends, their origins are still evident.

BOSCAWEN STREET c1955 T86013
This photograph shows the granite setts which still form the surface of Boscawen Street. Although many people refer to 'cobbled' streets, it is far more common to encounter setts - rectangular and regular - rather than true cobbles, which are rounded beach stones.

BOSCAWEN STREET c1960 T86042

The building on the site of the old Coinage Hall has been occupied by a series of banks. Tweedy's started off in 1848, and were followed by Capital and Counties, Lloyds (briefly, around 1923), the National Provincial after a fire in their premises next to the Red Lion, and eventually the Truro Savings Bank.

THE WAR MEMORIAL c1960 T86050

The War Memorial was unveiled on 15 October 1922 by the Lord Lieutenant of Cornwall, Mr C J Williams of Caerhays Castle. Also in attendance was the Mayor, Mr N B Bullen.

THE POST OFFICE c1955 T86032
Truro's old Post Office at High Cross was yet another building designed by Sylvanus Trevail. It was built on the site of the old Unicorn Inn in 1886; when it was eventually pulled down Marks and Spencer took over the site.

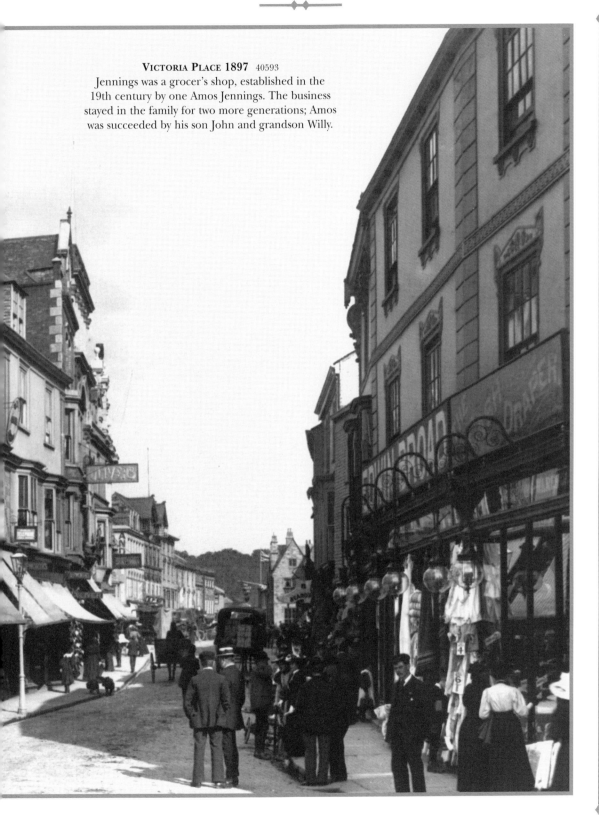

VICTORIA PLACE 1897 40593
Jennings was a grocer's shop, established in the
19th century by one Amos Jennings. The business
stayed in the family for two more generations; Amos
was succeeded by his son John and grandson Willy.

CATHEDRAL LANE c1960 T86052
Once known as Street Edy or Church Lane, Cathedral Lane links Boscawen Street and St Mary's Street. The Boscawen Street end is next to J Roberts.

KING STREET c1955 T86048

Like Boscawen Street, King Street has 18th- and 19th-century buildings and granite setts. In the background is Trevail's old Post Office.

PYDAR STREET c1955 T86033

On the right, just visible, is the Free Library, which opened in 1896. The money was provided by the noted philanthropist John Passmore Edwards, who also donated libraries in Falmouth, Launceston, Liskeard and Totnes. The architect, almost inevitably, was Trevail.

PYDAR STREET c1955 T86034

This view looks down Pydar Street towards King Street and the Post Office, with the Library hidden on the left. The cupola of Lloyd's Bank on Boscawen Street is just visible above the roofline.

PYDAR STREET c1955 T86035

The London Inn was demolished in the 1970s. The green and gold pub signs of the Devenish Brewery in Redruth were once common all over Devon and Cornwall, but the brewery closed down in the 1980s.

Index

Frith Book Co Titles

Frith Book Company publish over a 100 new titles each year. For latest catalogue please contact Frith Book Co.

Town Books 96pp, 100 photos. County and Themed Books 128pp, 150 photos (unless specified) All titles hardback laminated case and jacket except those indicated pb (paperback)

Around Barnstaple	1-85937-084-5	£12.99
Around Blackpool	1-85937-049-7	£12.99
Around Bognor Regis	1-85937-055-1	£12.99
Around Bristol	1-85937-050-0	£12.99
Around Cambridge	1-85937-092-6	£12.99
Cheshire	1-85937-045-4	£14.99
Around Chester	1-85937-090-X	£12.99
Around Chesterfield	1-85937-071-3	£12.99
Around Chichester	1-85937-089-6	£12.99
Cornwall	1-85937-054-3	£14.99
Cotswolds	1-85937-099-3	£14.99
Around Derby	1-85937-046-2	£12.99
Devon	1-85937-052-7	£14.99
Dorset	1-85937-075-6	£14.99
Dorset Coast	1-85937-062-4	£14.99
Around Dublin	1-85937-058-6	£12.99
East Anglia	1-85937-059-4	£14.99
Around Eastbourne	1-85937-061-6	£12.99
English Castles	1-85937-078-0	£14.99
Around Falmouth	1-85937-066-7	£12.99
Hampshire	1-85937-064-0	£14.99
Isle of Man	1-85937-065-9	£14.99
Around Maidstone	1-85937-056-X	£12.99
North Yorkshire	1-85937-048-9	£14.99
Around Nottingham	1-85937-060-8	£12.99
Around Penzance	1-85937-069-1	£12.99
Around Reading	1-85937-087-X	£12.99
Around St Ives	1-85937-068-3	£12.99
Around Salisbury	1-85937-091-8	£12.99
Around Scarborough	1-85937-104-3	£12.99
Scottish Castles	1-85937-077-2	£14.99
Around Sevenoaks and Tonbridge	1-85937-057-8	£12.99

Sheffield and S Yorkshire	1-85937-070-5	£14.99
Shropshire	1-85937-083-7	£14.99
Staffordshire	1-85937-047-0 (96pp)	£12.99
Suffolk	1-85937-074-8	£14.99
Surrey	1-85937-081-0	£14.99
Around Torbay	1-85937-063-2	£12.99
Wiltshire	1-85937-053-5	£14.99
Around Bakewell	1-85937-113-2	£12.99
Around Bournemouth	1-85937-067-5	£12.99
Cambridgeshire	1-85937-086-1	£14.99
Essex	1-85937-082-9	£14.99
Around Great Yarmouth	1-85937-085-3	£12.99
Hertfordshire	1-85937-079-9	£14.99
Isle of Wight	1-85937-114-0	£14.99
Around Lincoln	1-85937-111-6	£12.99
Oxfordshire	1-85937-076-4	£14.99
Around Shrewsbury	1-85937-110-8	£12.99
South Devon Coast	1-85937-107-8	£14.99
Around Stratford upon Avon	1-85937-098-5	£12.99
West Midlands	1-85937-109-4	£14.99

British Life A Century Ago
246 x 189mm
144pp, hardback.
Black and white
Lavishly illustrated with photos from the turn of the century, and with extensive commentary. It offers a unique insight into the social history and heritage of bygone Britain.

1-85937-103-5 £17.99

Available from your local bookshop or from the publisher

Around Bath	1-85937-097-7	£12.99	Mar
Cumbria	1-85937-101-9	£14.99	Mar
Down the Thames	1-85937-121-3	£14.99	Mar
Around Exeter	1-85937-126-4	£12.99	Mar
Greater Manchester	1-85937-108-6	£14.99	Mar
Around Harrogate	1-85937-112-4	£12.99	Mar
Around Leicester	1-85937-073-x	£12.99	Mar
Around Liverpool	1-85937-051-9	£12.99	Mar
Northumberland and Tyne & Wear			
	1-85937-072-1	£14.99	Mar
Around Oxford	1-85937-096-9	£12.99	Mar
Around Plymouth	1-85937-119-1	£12.99	Mar
Around Southport	1-85937-106-x	£12.99	Mar
Welsh Castles	1-85937-120-5	£14.99	Mar
Canals and Waterways	1-85937-129-9	£17.99	Apr
Around Guildford	1-85937-117-5	£12.99	Apr
Around Horsham	1-85937-127-2	£12.99	Apr
Around Ipswich	1-85937-133-7	£12.99	Apr
Ireland (pb)	1-85937-181-7	£9.99	Apr
London (pb)	1-85937-183-3	£9.99	Apr
New Forest	1-85937-128-0	£14.99	Apr
Around Newark	1-85937-105-1	£12.99	Apr
Around Newquay	1-85937-140-x	£12.99	Apr
Scotland (pb)	1-85937-182-5	£9.99	Apr
Around Southampton	1-85937-088-8	£12.99	Apr
Sussex (pb)	1-85937-184-1	£9.99	Apr
Around Winchester	1-85937-139-6	£12.99	Apr
Around Belfast	1-85937-094-2	£12.99	May
Colchester (pb)	1-85937-188-4	£8.99	May
Exmoor	1-85937-132-9	£14.99	May
Leicestershire (pb)	1-85937-185-x	£9.99	May
Lincolnshire	1-85937-135-3	£14.99	May
North Devon Coast	1-85937-146-9	£14.99	May
Nottinghamshire (pb)	1-85937-187-6	£9.99	May
Peak District	1-85937-100-0	£14.99	May
Around Truro	1-85937-147-7	£12.99	May
Yorkshire (pb)	1-85937-186-8	£9.99	May

Berkshire (pb)	1-85937-191-4	£9.99	Jun
Brighton (pb)	1-85937-192-2	£8.99	Jun
County Durham	1-85937-123-x	£14.99	Jun
Dartmoor	1-85937-145-0	£14.99	Jun
Down the Severn	1-85937-118-3	£14.99	Jun
East London	1-85937-080-2	£14.99	Jun
East Sussex	1-85937-130-2	£14.99	Jun
Glasgow (pb)	1-85937-190-6	£8.99	Jun
Kent (pb)	1-85937-189-2	£9.99	Jun
Kent Living Memories	1-85937-125-6	£14.99	Jun
Redhill to Reigate	1-85937-137-x	£12.99	Jun
Stone Circles & Ancient Monuments			
	1-85937-143-4	£17.99	Jun
Victorian & Edwardian Kent			
	1-85937-149-3	£14.99	Jun
Victorian & Edwardian Maritime Album			
	1-85937-144-2	£17.99	Jun
Victorian & Edwardian Yorkshire			
	1-85937-154-x	£14.99	Jun
West Sussex	1-85937-148-5	£14.99	Jun
Churches of Berkshire	1-85937-170-1	£17.99	Jul
Churches of Dorset	1-85937-172-8	£17.99	Jul
Derbyshire (pb)	1-85937-196-5	£9.99	Jul
Edinburgh (pb)	1-85937-193-0	£8.99	Jul
Folkstone	1-85937-124-8	£12.99	Jul
Gloucestershire	1-85937-102-7	£14.99	Jul
Herefordshire	1-85937-174-4	£14.99	Jul
North London	1-85937-206-6	£14.99	Jul
Norwich (pb)	1-85937-194-9	£8.99	Jul
Ports and Harbours	1-85937-208-2	£17.99	Jul
Somerset and Avon	1-85937-153-1	£14.99	Jul
South Devon Living Memories			
	1-85937-168-x	£14.99	Jul
Warwickshire (pb)	1-85937-203-1	£9.99	Jul
Worcestershire	1-85937-152-3	£14.99	Jul
Yorkshire Living Memories			
	1-85937-166-3	£14.99	Jul

FRITH PRODUCTS & SERVICES

Francis Frith would doubtless be pleased to know that the pioneering publishing venture he started in 1860 still continues today. More than a hundred and thirty years later, The Francis Frith Collection continues in the same innovative tradition and is now one of the foremost publishers of vintage photographs in the world. Some of the current activities include:

Interior Decoration

Today Frith's photographs can be seen framed and as giant wall murals in thousands of pubs, restaurants, hotels, banks, retail stores and other public buildings throughout the country. In every case they enhance the unique local atmosphere of the places they depict and provide reminders of gentler days in an increasingly busy and frenetic world.

Product Promotions

Frith products have been used by many major companies to promote the sales of their own products or to reinforce their own history and heritage. Brands include Hovis bread, Courage beers, Scots Porage Oats, Colman's mustard, Cadbury's foods, Mellow Birds coffee, Dunhill pipe tobacco, Guinness, and Bulmer's Cider.

Genealogy and Family History

As the interest in family history and roots grows world-wide, more and more people are turning to Frith's photographs of Great Britain for images of the towns, villages and streets where their ancestors lived; and, of course, photographs of the churches and chapels where their ancestors were christened, married and buried are an essential part of every genealogy tree and family album.

A series of easy-to-use CD Roms is planned for publication, and an increasing number of Frith photographs will be able to be viewed on specialist genealogy sites. A growing range of Frith books will be available on CD.

The Internet

Already thousands of Frith photographs can be viewed and purchased on the internet. By the end of the year 2000 some 60,000 Frith photographs will be available on the internet. The number of sites is constantly expanding, each focussing on different products and services from the Collection.

Some of the sites are listed below.

www.townpages.co.uk
www.icollector.com
www.barclaysquare.co.uk
www.cornwall-online.co.uk

For background information on the Collection look at the three following sites:

www.francisfrith.com
www.francisfrith.co.uk
www.frithbook.co.uk

Frith Products

All Frith photographs are available Framed or just as Mounted Prints, and can be ordered from the address below. From time to time other products - Address Books, Calendars, Table Mats, etc - are available.

> **For further information:**
> if you would like further information on any of the above aspects of the Frith business please contact us at the address below:
> **The Francis Frith Collection,**
> **Frith's Barn, Teffont, Salisbury, Wiltshire,**
> **England SP3 5QP.**
> Tel: +44 (0)1722 716 376 Fax: +44 (0)1722 716 881   Email: uksales@francisfrith.com

To receive your FREE Mounted Print

Mounted Print
Overall size 14 x 11 inches

Cut out this Voucher and return it with your remittance for £1.50 to cover postage and handling. Choose any photograph included in this book. Your SEPIA print will be A4 in size, and mounted in a cream mount with burgundy rule lines, overall size 14 x 11 inches.

Order additional Mounted Prints at HALF PRICE (only £7.49 each*)

If there are further pictures you would like to order, possibly as gifts for friends and family, acquire them at half price (no additional postage and handling required).

Have your Mounted Prints framed*

For an additional £14.95 per print you can have your chosen Mounted Print framed in an elegant polished wood and gilt moulding, overall size 16 x 13 inches (no additional postage and handling required).

---

* IMPORTANT!
These special prices are only available if ordered using the original voucher on this page (no copies permitted) and at the same time as your free Mounted Print, for delivery to the same address

---

Frith Collectors' Guild

From time to time we publish a magazine of news and stories about Frith photographs and further special offers of Frith products. If you would like 12 months FREE membership, please return this form.

Send completed forms to:
The Francis Frith Collection, Frith's Barn, Teffont, Salisbury, Wiltshire SP3 5QP

Voucher for FREE and Reduced Price Frith Prints

Picture no.	Page number	Qty	Mounted @ £7.49	Framed + £14.95	Total Cost
		1	**Free of charge***	£	£
			£7.49	£	£
			£7.49	£	£
			£7.49	£	£
			£7.49	£	£
			£7.49	£	£
			* Post & handling		£1.50
Book Title			**Total Order Cost**		£

Please do not photocopy this voucher. Only the original is valid, so please cut it out and return it to us.

I enclose a cheque / postal order for £ . . . .
made payable to 'The Francis Frith Collection'
OR please debit my Mastercard / Visa / Switch / Amex card

Number . . . .

Expires . . . . Signature . . . .

Name Mr/Mrs/Ms . . . .

Address . . . .

. . . .

. . . .

. . . . Postcode . . . .

Daytime Tel No . . . .   Valid to 31/12/01

The Francis Frith Collectors' Guild

Please enrol me as a member for 12 months free of charge.

Name Mr/Mrs/Ms . . . .

Address . . . .

. . . .

. . . .

. . . . Postcode . . . .

Free Print - see overleaf